SYNTHESIS SERIES

The spiritual director

A practical guide

D1571055

FRANCISCAN HERALD PRESS
1434 West 51st St. • Chicago, Ill. 60609

The Spiritual Director . . . A Practical Guide, by Damien Isabell O.F.M., S.T.D. Copyright © 1976 by Franciscan Herald Press, 1434 West 51st Street, Chicago, Illinois 60609.

ISBN: 8199-0712-X

Made in the United States of America.

NIHIL OBSTAT:

Mark Hegener O.F.M.
Censor

IMPRIMATUR:

Msgr. Richard A. Rosemeyer, J.D.
Vicar General, Archdiocese of Chicago

May 24, 1976

"The Nihil Obstat and the Imprimatur are official declarations that a book or pamphlet is free of doctrinal or moral error. No implication is contained therein that those who have granted the Nihil Obstat and Imprimatur agree with the contents, opinions or statements expressed."

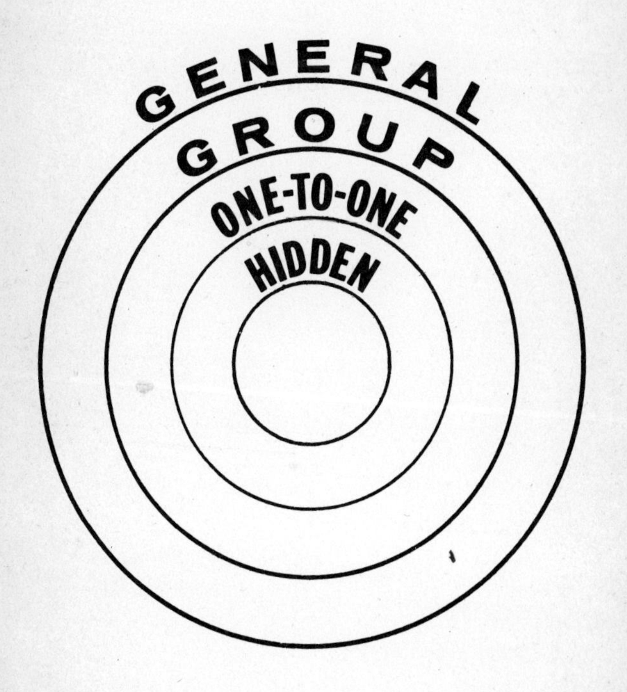
GENERAL
GROUP
ONE-TO-ONE
HIDDEN

CONTENTS

General Editor Introduction 5

Introduction 8

Acknowledgments 9

Chapter I
Direction and Spirituality 11

Chapter II
Group Direction: Institutional Director/Spiritual Father 19

Chapter III
Surrounded by a Cloud of Witnesses 24

Chapter IV
Jump Right In 29

Chapter V
Counseling or Spiritual Direction? Woe is Me! 31

Chapter VI
A Tender Trap 35

Chapter VII
Draw the Water from the Fountain Within....39

Chapter VIII
Where two or three are together, there am I" — The Interview 42

Chapter IX
Core of Direction 53

Chapter X
Guidance in Prayer 58

Chapter XI
Directions of Direction 63

Chapter XII
Bibliography 68

EDITORIAL PREFACE

THE AIM OF SYNTHESIS SERIES

As the growing edge of knowledge increases its pace and widens the domain of man, new vistas strike us which are both exciting and frightening. Although the spreading light reveals more and more the marvels of our universe, still the bordering darkness of the unknown expands along with it.

Nowhere is the uncharted field of the universe of being more deeply felt today than in the area which concerns man himself. Here especially our growing knowledge deepens awareness of the vast unknown beyond our present range of vision.

We have begun to realize that the project of comprehending man is indeed gigantic. It is the conviction of all who seriously contemplate the problem that only a multi-disciplinary approach and synthesis will produce a true picture. We find emerging a cooperative effort by those engaged in any discipline which bears upon understanding man and promoting his well-being. The human sciences, the arts, philosophy, religion and all the helping arts reveal him in the several dimensions of his complex pattern of life.

SYNTHESIS SERIES is intended to introduce the reader to the experience of using the multi-disciplinary approach when attempting to understand himself and others. We believe this will lead to his perceiving and relating to the entire human family more effectively — that is, more in accord with rich depth and breadth of all those realities it contains. We hope this will help reduce the confusion caused by the over-simplified "answers" to problems of living which used to be offered by specialists in various fields.

Instead of the easy or quick answers we propose that each individual make steady serious effort to achieve a rich synthesis of concepts developed by many disciplines. This appears to be the only method that holds the promise of yielding the fundamental answer— the meaning his own existence is supposed to have — a meaning so often fretfully and falteringly sought by everyone whether he admits it or not. The promise and its realization in personal experience provide sufficient motive to undertake and sustain the search. But beyond this, one can foresee benefits which transcend individual well-being. For personal growth of many individuals brings about a **social atmosphere** which stimulates still further development toward a more meaningful life on the part of each member of the group.

This interaction between an individual and others is apparent when we observe the opposite process of deterioration. Just as the most disruptive factor in society is the unrest caused by failure of its members to find the meaning of life, so the reverse holds true, that society will benefit at all levels in proportion to the success people have in their quest for the meaning they believe their existence is supposed to have.

SYNTHESIS SERIES, we repeat, is intended to introduce the reader to the new multi-disciplinary method in carrying out the search for the meaning his life is to have when viewed in reference to the destiny of mankind.

INTRODUCTION

This booklet is the fruit of my work with the Midwest Association of Spiritual Directors, that excellent organization of fellow directors whose lives are so encouraging.

There are many excellent books and articles on spiritual direction, but unfortunately, they are not readily available to the man or woman in the field. This booklet attempts to fill that need. It does not pretend to be a manual which touches all questions on direction. Rather, it will fulfill its purposes if a) its readers understand more clearly just how their work fits in the work of the Church, b) the readers become acquainted with some of the available literature, c) the directors are lead to study more in depth some of the points merely touched upon.

All comments will be welcomed by people in the field who might want to see a second edition containing the fruit of their own observations and resources.

ACKNOWLEDGMENTS

Special gratitude must be extended to those brothers who wrote me letters of criticism before I redid this edition. To these and the many others who shared their experiences with me, thanks: Bob Lenz, Jerry Neufelder, Blaise Hettich, John R. Reuscher, Ed Bell, Rudy Breunig, John Czyzynski, Gerry Pecht, Jim Strommer, Frank Wittouck and Al Krupp. I hope they will notice that I took their suggestions seriously.

DEDICATED TO MY PARENTS
IN GRATITUDE

DAMIEN ISABELL O.F.M.

I
DIRECTION AND SPIRITUALITY

In a recent article, Adrian van Kaam distinguishes between what he correctly calls *fundamental* spirituality from what are considered *special* spiritualities. The first is "the study and practice of those necessary and sufficient conditions that make possible the development of any spiritual life whatever . . ." He is contrasting this with spiritualities such as Ignatian, Augustinian, Franciscan, Montfortan which are "valid insofar as they contain also the necessary and sufficient conditions." Today more than ever we are forced to "sort out" what is happening in the field of spirituality and this distinction is very helpful. Any serious director will attempt to remain open to new developments while always remaining rooted in what is central. We will speak of these fundamentals later on. At present we simply make an appeal to each director to enunciate for himself or herself what is truly basic in their understanding of the spiritual life? This articulation is the first step to being an effective director.

Another helpful distinction is made between *spiritual direction* and *spiritual self-direction.* The former we speak about when we say: "I spend five hours a day giving spiritual direction," or "I am a spiritual director." *Spiritual self-direction* is based on the assumption that the core of man's self is his spirit "and the primary force of man's unfolding is his spirituality. Spiritualization implies surrender to the transcendent and the discovery and acceptance of one's unique spiritual life-direction in the light of the transcendent. Spiritualization entails, secondly, the incarnation of one's spiritual life-direction in the personal and vital aspects of one's total self." Van Kaam wants to take our attention off of the role of director since it can never substitute for the personal discovery of the direction implanted by God within each one's heart. The gradual uncovering of that direction will determine how any particular individual will concretize his life. A spiritual director will simply be at the service of the person's self-direction.

With these distinctions in mind, we can turn to a reflection on the models of direction operative within the church.

Four Basic Models

If we were to draw four concentric circles, we could graphically situate our understanding of spiritual direction. For lack of a better term we call the outermost circle "the general direction of the Church"; the next inner circle is "institutional or group direction"; the third circle "one-to-one direction"; and, finally, the innermost circle we call "hidden direction.' We are looking at direction from the outside in order to make a typology. What is comprised in each of these types of direction?

General direction of the Church means that the Church itself is the fundamental spiritual director. She organizes her teaching, morality and rituals in order to direct the attention of her children towards the Lord. In her catechumenate she sets the foundation of the direction along which she will lead her people; in the word, sacraments and liturgical year she realizes what she preaches and sustains her people in their direction toward the Lord. No special spirituality can negate or neglect this direction as the very foundation on which it is built. This general direction unites all Christians.

We called the second circle *institutional or group direction.* This term includes all groups within the church formed to profit more fully from the general direction of the Church. Some of these groups are "institutions of total direction" such as monasteries, seminaries or other structured ways of living Christian life. Every detail of their life is oriented towards profiting from the spiritual richness present within the Church (e.g. silence in order to assimilate God's word). Other groups are less tightly knit, but they also use particular ascetical means which will enable them to grow in their union with God and to take greater advantage of the richness of the Church's direction. Examples of such groups would be: retreat houses, Marriage Encounter, House Church Movement, Cursillo, Focolare, priests' support groups, etc.

One-to-one direction is what we ordinarily think of when we speak of spiritual direction. For the most part this has been restricted to a very select group of people throughout history. I would venture to propose that it is needed on a more general level at those times when the general direction of the Church is weak, symbolically poor, when the word of God as preached does not address real life, when there is great ambiguity in theology and when there has been a certain compromise with worldly values. Much of our discussion in this pamphlet will be centered on this type of direction.

Finally, there are those whom van Kaam calls *hidden directors*. These are represented by the central circle of our concentric circles. "To find ourselves we need to follow the reactions and responses of fellow human beings to the life directives we are manifesting by our behavior . . . This experience of worthwhile directedness of life is the foundation for the later graces experience of being lovingly appreciated by God himself as called by him to a unique spiritual direction." Heroes evoke admiration, "a willingness to perceive that there is someone greater than I and a willingness to invite them in." Some of these directors have exercised a very positive influence on our lives, whether we consciously recognize them or not; others have, on the contrary, influenced us negatively, whether we are conscious of this or not.

Each of these models deserve a longer treatment for all the direction we do will somehow be within these four areas.

— 1 —

Returning to the *general direction* of the Church, we are forced to deal with liturgical spirituality as explained by G. Braso, OSB in *Liturgy and Spirituality.* Christian spirituality is not dependent on the theory of any one author. The *magisterium* of the Church has been entrusted with revealed doctrine and no school may create a new spirituality different from the Church's. "Where doctrine is concerned, the Church exercises her *magisterium* authoritatively and by herself, whether in the determination of revealed truth or in anything pertaining to the norms of morality directed toward the attainment of the supernatural end." Since the Church "is to reproduce and actualize in time the mystery of Jesus Christ; she is to communicate the knowledge of that mystery to men; and she is to insert vitally into that mystery the life of every Christian"; she must have a particular method for doing so.

The Church's method has two aspects: private spiritual activity is considered a preparation for liturgical celebration, and private spiritual activity is seen as a vital assimilation of the liturgy. This emphasis on the centrality of the Church's teaching, on the sacraments, and on the liturgical year are permanent voices which call Christians out of the traps of a purely subjective piety which feels constrained to create everything anew. Day by day the Church both reveals the mystery of Christ in word, symbol and action and more fully incorporates her people into that mystery which is

Christ alive in our midst. Fasting and rejoicing, contemplation and action, teachings and symbols, reading and listening, common prayer and private prayer, receiving and giving — all are elements of the Church's direction. "To orient all things to God, not only in so far as this worship tends to unite us to him, the liturgy reduces everything to the supreme motif of charity, and centers its worshipful and educational activity in the Eucharist, which is the sacrifice of Christ's charity, the sacrament of union with God and of brotherly communion" (Braso, 184).

— 2 —

An example will illustrate well what we mean by group direction. The Better World Movement has distributed a paper entitled "Dimensions to Dialogue" which suggests some very valuable procedures for building up the body of Christ, which is the thrust of the Eucharist itself. In order to make that grace more operative, however, this paper speaks of five exercises which a community can use in order to grow up together in Christ. *Shared prayer* is the way of growing in an ability to share life. "Shared prayer provides an opportunity for Christians to experience community life at the deepest possible level — that point where man enters into intimate contact with God." *Communication of life* is the second step the group is to take after the first step has become comfortable for all. "As this mutual respect and trust of the good will of the other grows we can reveal more of our deep concerns, our feelings, our desires, our ambitions about our personal lives as Christians." The next step is *revision of apostolate* for "every Christian community must ask itself constantly how well it is fulfilling this mission." Passing from external works, the community then passes to the *revision of community* during the course of which it asks itself: what does community mean to me? how do I see myself as a member of this community? what do I expect from this community? what do I expect to give to this community? On this foundation *fraternal correction,* the fifth step, will be possible. It promotes the circulation of love and truth within the community. This is one method. Each group, each institution will have its own "way." What is common, however, is that each one organizes its activity in order to profit more fully from the general direction of the Church. By means of this commitment they also identify themselves with the Church's self-direction, its constant orientation towards Christ.

Seminary direction is a form of group direction and I would like to call the readers' attention to the *Cara Seminary Forum* which did a study on "Spiritual Formation" in 1972. Those who answered the questionnaire sent by Cara claimed that the Eucharist, a personal spiritual director, and prayer in common and private were the three most basic elements of any seminary spiritual formation program. In the very next breath the question of the distinctive needs of the seminarians was discussed: positive self-image, need for acceptance, sense of value, help in dealing with the uncertainty "caused by constant change and to adjust to the inhospitable evaluation of the Church and of the priesthood by the world today, especially by its youth." This interplay between the "fundamental" and the "special" gives rise to the perennial questions of evaluation, freedom, accountability, privacy, pluralism (do we all have to go to Mass?), and integration. These are complex issues which can only be dealt with by a team. In the bibliography I have indicated some helpful literature.

— 3 —

One-to-one direction can take many forms. It can be short term or long term. Short term direction is ordinarily described as "problem solving." A sister is having difficulty in community, a young man is having trouble with masturbation, a contemplative needs help in prayer. Long term direction is based on a contract between the director and directee. It is concerned with the discovery of one's self-direction and thus will require a rather stable, long term relationship during the course of which the directee will let the director know just who he is, with his past, present, and future dimensions, what he wants to be, and how he or she interprets all of this in the light of faith. This booklet will explain more in detail all of these elements.

— 4 —

Hidden directors are present everywhere in our lives and little need be said about them. God in his goodness is always directing us in our daily lives and it is simply up to us to discover this guidance.

A final note calls our attention to the fact that Jesus worked primarily with groups by his preaching, teaching and example. At the same time he made himself available for a more intimate one-to-one relationship in moments of crisis. It is the opinion of van Kaam that we should spend more time giving good group direction which would inspire others to seek their own direction rather than concentrating so much effort on one-to-one direction which will never be available to all Christians by the very limitations of well-prepared personnel.

II

GROUP DIRECTION: INSTITUTIONAL DIRECTOR/SPIRITUAL FATHER

An institutional director is a group director whose main concern is to provide an environment in which ministers for the Church will find all they need to develop and test their spiritual lives and vocation. I find it helpful to clarify the distinction between the persons who do this kind of direction from those who are "charismatic directors" such as the fathers of the desert. Whereas the work of an institutional director is important, it is rarely of the intensity or depth of one deeply experienced in the mystical ways of prayer and penance. The former is more closely connected with education and can use all the information available on good educational procedures, the second is more personal and pertains to the science of mysticism. With this in mind, we can ask the question . . .

Why have you been chosen spiritual director? Because you have a degree in counseling? Or do you work well with people? Perhaps you have studied spirituality, or the bishop likes you. Then it is possible that you have been a good priest, Brother or Sister and your superiors have confidence in you. Or maybe no one else wanted the job . . .

In any case, welcome aboard. You are not alone, as St. Peter said. You have brothers and sisters throughout the whole world sharing your same burden. But remember that your yoke will be sweeter and your burden lighter if you can see clearly just what job you have been given.

It would be a terrible burden to step into the sandals of the "spiritual fathers" of old. As a matter of fact, from the reaction I hear among many directors, I suspect that they see their role in the light of these venerable spiritual masters and are therefore terrified. "What do I know about the spiritual life?" is the inevitable first reply.

My suspicion is that a man chosen to be a spiritual director is proof enough that he is qualified to be an institutional director but maybe not a spiritual father in the traditional sense of the term. Allow me to explain this distinction.

The institutional or canonical director is described in paragraph one of canon 1360 which speaks of "priests who are outstanding, not only for their sound doctrine, but also for their virtues and prudence, who can benefit the students by word and example." Elsewhere he is described as a "specialist in spiritual matters just as the other professors are in their subjects." What is being said here and what is reiterated in Vatican II is that the institution wants and chooses men who are mature Christians, who have experience in the spiritual life and who can share it with others, and who are truly Catholic in every sense of the word.

This is a far cry from the image of the gaunt ascetic waiting in his cave for a novice to come to him with some diabolical temptation or some mystical state. To put it in other words, the canonical director is the best representative of the institution which he serves; the desert father is decisively charismatic, one who will represent the unique grace God has given him. We will come back to this.

If the director is at the service of the Church, then he is the one who will be responsible for providing the environment in which the candidates can come to know and experience all that is best in the spiritual tradition of the Church. Traditionally he has had public duties (conferences, days of recollection, personal spiritual direction). At evaluation time he or she is painfully aware that this latter area is the most important for he has "the duty to know the life and character of the seminarians so as to be able to give them prudent and safe guidance regarding their vocation. Those who should not continue to the priesthood, because they have not been called, he will dissuade from their intention of becoming priests, but those who are true to their calling he will encourage to ever greater efforts towards perfection."

This does not mean that the officially appointed director will always be the most apt one to help the students make their vocational decision. It is quite possible that some faculty member or some other person will have a special gift in this regard. Then he or she must have the humility to recognize this and to direct the individual to the person who can be of true service. This does not mean that the director is a failure. His very important job is to provide the atmosphere in which Christ's love will reach everyone. At times this will mean moving forward, at other times it will demand stepping back. At all times it means being there so Christ's presence can be felt.

This service is directed towards aiding candidates for the ministry to make a decision according to God's will. "Is this person called to minister as an ordained person or a consecrated religious?" Here spiritual direction is at the service of the institutional ministry.

In contrast, we have the type of person who is called "a spiritual father" or "a spiritual mother." Much as this terminology seems antiquated, it bears a profound significance in the history of spirituality. These are the holy persons who have been tried in the desert, persons who are full of wisdom and single-minded confidence because they have totally surrendered themselves to God's loving will. There is no longer any question of a frantic search for power or position. By now this person is beyond the temptation to seek social acceptance. He or she is one who is at peace with his past and the people who inhabit it, with his present and the people who fill it and with his future. Merton says that such a "father" or "abba" is one who does not live with "aggressive and hostile fantasies," for he has discovered his heart. After a long and exacting apprenticeship under another "abba," he has finally become one with himself, his God and others.

The spiritual father is not appointed, nor is he or she necessarily a priest or a religious. If he is in charge of others, it is only because they have come to him because of his personal, spiritual authority. When he does give guidance, he is concerned with helping the individual unmask his self-deceptions in order to be completely receptive to God's instruction. Bring men back to objective reality and away from a deceptive fantasy life is much more important than helping an individual make a decision for the ministry after his fourth year of theology, though this is not necessarily excluded.

In the seminary situation or in formation work on any level, we can get very discouraged if we expect to have a relationship with each candidate as intense as that between a "spiritual father" and his novice. We can hardly presume to have their spiritual authority. What we can fall back on, and feel comfortable with, is the fact that we have been sent, commissioned by the Church for our service. This means that we are constantly backed up by the Spirit acting through the Word and through our love. As institutional directors we are not "gurus" in competition with the masters of the Orient. Very simply, we have been found worthy to serve for a time in the capacity of guide. We direct our care for Christ toward those who are entrusted to us and we use our talents, spiritual experience and knowledge to serve those who are looking for themselves and God.

III
SURROUNDED BY A CLOUD OF WITNESSES

Of course you understand that you are not the first one to work in a seminary or to be a spiritual director. We can get a feel for the tradition in which we stand when we quickly review the institutional history of direction.

Jesus spent much time forming his disciples,

teaching them how to pray and helping them reform their attitudes toward the law, the poor, the rich, the kingdom, power, position and so forth. Following suit, the apostles were careful about those on whom they laid hands. One might say that every bishop was a spiritual director who examined the good dispositions and the life-style of each person who wished to minister in the Church of God (II Tim 2, 22-26; I Tim 5, 22; 3, 10). As time went on, more formal instruction was imparted to candidates in the catechetical schools. Nonetheless, these did not wholly substitute for the formation under the bishops direction; candidates had to be known by him and had to prove themselves mature.

Eventually monasteries were used for the training of the clergy, especially in the West. With these came the notion of seclusion, prayer schedule and regular schooling. It is presumed that the spiritual direction given the monks was also conferred on candidates for the clergy. It is good to remember at this point that neither the catechetical school nor the monastery were the only places for spiritual or intellectual formation.

St. Augustine is generally considered the one who blended monasticism and clerical life in a happy union. In his monastery near the episcopal residence, he trained his clergy and provided the Church with many well-trained bishops. Out of this idea grew the so-called *episcopia,* schools directed by the bishop in which the young would be preserved from the evil of society and from the passion society experienced. Pope Gregory had a famous school at St. John Lateran in Rome.

In more rural areas, priestly formation and spiritual direction took place in rectory schools. Here the local pastor would gather promising youth around himself and prepare them to exercise their minor orders and to prepare well for the reception of major orders. By 766, parallel institutions were set up in the city under the guidance of canons regular. St. Chrodegang of Metz is the name to remember here. Likewise, Charlemagne devoted much of his time to the education of the clergy. Candidates had to be thirty years old before they could be ordained, legislation which goes back to the fourth century, and they had to be under the guidance of holy teachers.

When clerical formation was brought to the university scene, intellectual preparation improved and spiritual guidance all but disappeared. It is the opinion of Sackett and others, (see bibliography) that the few who did frequent the university were almost totally secularized "which is amply borne out by the legislation of the times which was directed at the return of religious to their monasteries and of clerics to their own schools."

St. Ignatius was the spiritual director who had the genius of being able to organize what we would call today "seminaries." In 1551, he founded the Roman College and in 1552, the German. He was able to combine the best of the monastic tradition of spiritual guidance with the demands of the institution. He stressed personal contact with the students and appointed one man as director. In 1563, Trent adopted Ignatius' plan for the whole Church in its famous decree "Cum adolescentium aetas." Daily Mass, monthly confession and communion were prescribed for the young candidates.

St. Charles Borromeo was the one who put into reality Trent's prescriptions. In Milan, he opened seminaries and entrusted them to the Jesuits. These expert directors, however, attracted more vocations to their own Order, so very soon St. Charles formed an Order of diocesan priests who would follow the same basic plan of Jesuit formation. Thus, there were mental prayer, examination of conscience, sacramental life, conquering of self, mortification of the passions and practice of virtues, fidelity to ecclesiastical laws and, of course, the retreat under the guidance of one's confessor, who prepared meditations for the candidate and prepared him for the sacrament. In these seminaries on man was named as spiritual director.

To be complete in our historical survey, we should study Ven. Bartholomew Holzhauser (1613-1658), St. Vincent de Paul, who had already begun his recollection days for the clergy by 1635, and St. John Eudes (1601-1681). But since our space is limited we will mention briefly M. Olier, founder of the Sulpicians, since their practice of spiritual direction was appreciably different than the Jesuit. Instead of having one spiritual director, the seminary had four directors and the superior. The latter assigned a director to each seminarian, who was supposed to consult with him every 15 days or once a month. This luxury could hardly continue after the French Revolution because of the lack of priests, so the spiritual directors also took on the job of teaching. This created many problems if only because of the time factor.

By the time of the Code, two traditions of seminary direction were widespread. The first stemmed from St. Ignatius who wanted one director. The "Roman system," as it was called, offered:

> the advantage of an eminently capable priest who devotes all his time to this essential function; unity of direction is assured; there is no chance of the director using his influence in the disciplinary field either for or against his penitents . . . The only objection was that the spiritual director did not always reside at the seminary . . .

The second tradition of the Sulpicians was called the "French system." This gave:

> greater liberty of choice; better direction was assured in that each director was further enlightened as to his penitents by the comments of the others made in council meetings; each director had more time to give to his penitents, since the number was limited, and ordinarily bi-monthly direction was customary . . . The disadvantages were that not all professors have the age, prudence, experience and knowledge of mystical and ascetical theology to suit them for this difficult task; not all have time for it, if they are to try to do justice to their classes . . .

From history a few salient points come forth clearly: spiritual guidance must be provided for those who will be charged with guiding others, those who provide this direction must be mature and prepared, the spiritual director is to deal in the internal forum, and many of the questions that arise will stem from this tension between internal and external forum, finally a spiritual director must have time to devote to his directees.

You are now on the list of spiritual directors, you are surrounded by a cloud of witnesses who had to struggle with the same questions you will face. At times like this, faith in the communion of saints is consoling and encouraging.

IV
JUMP RIGHT IN

The new director begins with caution and uncertainty. Perhaps he or she does not yet realize that no seminary or order has ever created a perfectly planned formation program. In trash barrels throughout the world he can find plans of previous disasters . . . and successes. Nevertheless, each try has helped someone.

Today much of the isolation felt by the spiritual director of the past is overcome by his ability to work with a team. Whether alone or as a team, the director must keep the basic question in mind: Are our structures providing "spiritual training . . . in such a way that the student might learn to live in intimate and unceasing union with the Father, through his Son Jesus Christ in the Holy Spirit" (*Decree on Priestly Formation,* 8). If we are honest with ourselves, we recognize how we have come to know Christ Jesus through the guidance of others. We appreciate the fact that growth did not just happen, that it required a lot of focusing in on certain areas of life and it demanded a lot of effort to arrive at self-knowledge and knowledge of Christ.

The underlying presumption is that spiritual life does not just happen. A poor understanding of "non-directive guidance" can destroy all confidence in one's ability to do something to promote growth. We who are priests or religious have something to share and we would like to communicate this to others. In formation work our lives are as important as the programs we concoct, for they reveal basic attitudes, peace and integration which are the values sought by those who come to us.

Perhaps we can use the idea of "care" to explain how we should go about our work. In this regard, I highly suggest the small paperback book by Milton Mayeroff, entitled *On Caring,* (Perennial Library). "To help another person grow," says the author, "is at least to help him to care for something or someone apart from himself, and it involves encouraging and assisting him to find and create areas of his own in which he is able to care. Also, it is to help that other person to come to care for himself, and by becoming responsive to his own need to care to become responsible for his own life." Others need us to grow out of their immature self-seeking, into the freedom of reality. If the director is able to manifest by his life the care he has for Christ, the Church and for this individual or group, he will inevitably be raising the question in the minds of others, "Why? What is making him tick? What is giving him his joy and power?" Then on the level of faith the director can help one learn how to care for Christ in his own way.

V

COUNSELING OR SPIRITUAL DIRECTION? WOE IS ME!

An example: A seminarian in his college years feels under much tension. He has an exaggerated fear of failure in his academic work (so he overstudies) and in his pastoral work (so he overworks). He is very uncomfortable when he is not doing something. Consequently his prayer life is at a stand-still, for he cannot stand still. In simple terms, this young man is not functioning well, he is all taken up in some partial aspect of his life (success/work), he is out of dialogue with the real world. He could use counseling. Under counseling he will discover what image he has of himself and what it is doing to him. Some excellent examples of how individuals can distort the wholeness of their lives can be found in the *must* book by W. Kraft, *The Search for the Holy,* (Westminster Press).

A rule of thumb is that a person needs counseling when he or she is absorbed in some partial aspect of life. I say "absorbed" to indicate that the individual is preoccupied with this to such an extent that other values or aspects of life are neglected. He does not "feel at home" or "feel comfortable" with his superior, for example, because he feels threatened by authority. He does not "feel comfortable" spending time in prayer because of his exaggerated need to belong or to accomplish. Or he has developed a habit of masturbation because he is afraid to assume the demands of relationships in the adult world.

The spiritual director regards every person with optimism. He knows that Christ has come to bring abundant life, and abundant life means openness to the whole of reality. At times the director himself will be able to help the person understand what is happening to him. Through his care, he may very well be able to help the person understand how he relates to the whole world in partial ways. In this regard, Kraft's book is a most useful tool, for it helps one see most clearly the three ways that we all relate to reality.

The body way is the spontaneous, pre-reflective

way. Because of our imbeddedness in the world, we cannot live simply with thoughts, projects or contemplation. It is imperative to listen to one's body, for the body speaks. On the other hand, the body is impulsive and selfish: "in itself [it] strives for immediate relief and will blindly use anything or anybody to achieve its pleasure."

The ego way of relating to the world is the rational approach, by means of reflective thinking and willing. This is man the manager, the one who is task-oriented, who wants to get something done. On the one hand, the value of the ego is that it enables one to accomplish something in life and to organize life in a meaningful way. On the other hand, the person whose whole life is ego directed will have no time for relaxation, will not be able to be alone, will have to control everything and everyone.

The third way of relating to reality is termed the "self" approach. Here I experience reality in terms of wonder, or in terms of being united with it having no desire to control or abuse it. As self, I respect the other person as unique, "I have no need to manipulate or dominate him, nor do I need to seduce him to satisfy my own needs. I am not seduced by his sensuality, nor do I analyze him." When we say that a person should be "open," we are speaking of this dimension of the person where freedom and love are found.

A person can exaggerate any of these ways. One cannot always live unreflectively nor can he always seek his satisfaction. Likewise, man is not meant to be a manager twenty-four hours a day, forgetting the demands of his body, forgetting the rights of others, forgetting his need for beauty and for prayer. But then neither can one pray all day nor dialogue all day to discover love. If the spiritual direction cannot help a person see how he or she is living a partial life, or if he cannot help him move to greater balance, then he should use the services of a professional counselor.

Thus, counseling wants to foster attitudes which will help the person function better in his concrete, visible, day to day world. It is an attempt to put him back in contact with his total world so that he can manage his life better and more efficiently. With this as a foundation, spiritual direction is concerned with seeing the total world in the light of God's plan of salvation. It says that one's total world includes God as well, and that the Spirit of God is trying to share God's life with each person. In direction, both director and directee stand before God discovering his loving plan and not being afraid to uncover one's own sinfulness, one's own selfish refusal of God's gift of love. Spiritual direction helps the individual foster attitudes which will help the person relate more personally and more deeply with his hidden God and his brothers here on earth. Counseling presumes honesty, spiritual direction presumes faith as well.

Much of what follows should clarify this distinction even more. Let's move on to one element now that is common to both direction and counseling.

VI
A TENDER TRAP

Transference is a technical term for "the redirection of feelings and desires and especially of those unconsciously retained from childhood toward a new object (as a psychoanalyst conducting therapy.)" Van Kaam has a very positive development of this phenomenon in chapter three of his book, *Religion and Personality.* On the positive side of the ledger, "Each of my transferences may help me to grow by means of a temporary identification with the values embodied in the particular person or institution." I like this way of explaining the process, for transference is not limited only to the counseling or spiritual direction relationship. Since man's deepest desire is for God alone, and since man does not realize this, he looks for other people or things which temporarily take the place of God.

All this happens unconsciously. Since each person in a relationship has a whole network of unsatisfied needs, it is very easy to understand why one would always be searching to fulfill these needs and would pounce on the person or situation which promised fulfillment.

> It may be that my parents did not take loving and consistent care of the needs of my helpless body. In this case, it will be difficult for me to go beyond the narcissistic orientation of my

> religious drive because the absence of loving and consistent care made me overanxious. I became so concerned about my survival . . . that I cannot believe it is safe to give up my preoccupation with my own needs. I do not dare to forget myself even for a moment and to really enjoy the presence of others.

Because of the intimacy of the relationship, the spiritual director is inevitably one of those objects toward which feelings and desires are going to be directed. Ordinarily he or she is a caring person, a celibate, a holy person, a competent person, a person with authority. Many will be seeking security, a non-threatening sexual relationship, separation from the dirtiness of life, a person with all the answers, or finally, someone whom they can obey. The inexperienced director can easily accept this transference and maintain the relationship on its basis alone. For example, he can constantly give advice and answers to the directee, never allowing him to make his own decisions. Or instead of listening to what is really being said by the person, the director can be easily seduced by stories of woe. True care for the person requires that the director accept the identification, but then gradually lead the person beyond it. The director in a minor seminary will be a surrogate father for awhile, but it would be unfair to allow this relationship to continue as such just because the director has an unfulfilled need for a son, or for affection or for success.

Liberation from this seduction, or rather, living through it and not stopping at it, is part of the process of spiritual growth. Eventually all this stops in the partial will, and will bring the person to realize that in "no-thing" is God found and that the solitude, lonliness, anxiety and guilt that I experience are found the *humus* out of which develops my relationship with God. Francis of Assisi literally had no-thing, and yet was able to say "My God and my All."

How can the director know whether or not he has been "sucked in" by the idolization of his directee? Many have found helpful the following evamination from a A. Godin's book, *The Priest as Counselor* (Divine Word Publications). I should suspect myself of displaying a tendency toward the transferential aspect of a relationship if I:

1. feel uneasy, sad or depressed, or on the contrary, elated, enthusiastic or excited about the counselee;
2. experience sudden waves of enthusiasm or boredom during our meetings;
3. have long impassioned arguments with him;
4. feel worried by his reproaches or criticisms;
5. derive enormous conscious pleasure from his congratulations, his signs of satisfaction, gratitude or affection;
6. am incapable of refusing to adopt the expected attitude (e.g. reassurance, praise, encouragement, friendship);
7. steer the conversation away from certain subjects which he brings up (e.g. death, sexual experience, money);
8. maintain a continuous dependence in the counseling relationship, especially by the

constant use of reassuring w o r d s and phrases;

9. encourage the counselee in his aggressive self-release from a relationship against which he is rebelling (e.g. against his family, his community, his wife or employer);
10. feel obligated to help him by interfering in the details of his daily life, by taking the initiative in his place (e.g. by phoning the doctor) or by easily resolving problems by the use of personal influence;
11. am careless about the practical details of our meetings, or take unusual pains over them (e.g. punctuality, choice of room, arrangements for the next meeting);
12. make a point of discussing his case with my colleagues, emphasizing his importance, his merits or his personality;
13. talk about him in an ironic or cynical manner;
14. worry continually about the successful outcome of his case, about whether he is following my advice, and about keeping in contact with him;
15. dream about him.

My remarks are not meant to be a course in counseling. They might point to something actual in your work. If they do, talk things over with experienced directors. I also highly recommend chapter three of Godin's book which gives some very useful advice on how to bring to successful resolution this process of transference.

VII

DRAW THE WATER FROM THE FOUNTAIN WITHIN (JN. 4, 14)

To use the terminology of chapter four, priests and other professionals are quite taken up with ego operations. They are used to finding labels, to controlling and classifying, explaining and organizing. As soon as we have said something about transference, we must quickly speak about listening. Listening sounds more passive than counselling or directing, yet it pertains to the essence of both. If one is a preacher he will naturally seek an audience; if he is a teacher he will seek students; if he is a plumber he will seek pipes. The spiritual director is one who puts himself at the service of the activity of the Holy Spirit, so he must seek the Spirit.

A spiritual director can presume that the Spirit of God is working in the heart of each directee. Even more, he believes that God has been leading that individual for many years and that the director is now invited to see what God has wrought. The greatest service the director can render the one who seeks his help is that of truly hearing what he is trying to say, so that the Spirit working within him can release His saving power. This means that the director must recognize and control his compulsive desire to speak and to classify; he must learn to be comfortable with periods of silence; he must try not to be preoccupied with a desire for success or with a concern for meeting all the requirements of a good interview.

Listening is at the service of knowing. "To care for someone, I must know many things. I must know, for example, who the other is, what his powers and limitations are, what his needs are, and what is conducive to his growth; I must know how to respond to his needs, and what my own powers and limitations are." The director knows what the spiritual life is, but in direction, he must know what the spiritual life of this individual is. The knowledge he will attain of him will be explicit, for it will be able to be verbalized, and implicit, for he will know more about him than what he can verbalize. Again, he may come to know something is so without being able to deal with it, just as he can know the person directly as existing in his own right, or he can simply have information about the person.

In all these cases, listening skills need to be developed. An exercise that might prove helpful to the beginning director is the writing of a verbatim. This is a word by word account of the interview, with the felt reactions of the participants. By recalling a particular session with a directee, and by writing it down in this way, the director will be able to see whether or not he had actually listened and heard what was being said or had missed the point completely. Better yet, change the names and circumstances and have a colleague or a professional counselor read it and make his observations. In this way we express our own accountability to our directees.

Role playing sessions with your fellow spiritual directors can also be broadening experiences. This can be done very simply. Bring in a number of cases that will not reveal any confidences. One person will take the role of the directee and will present his problem to another who is playing the director. Meanwhile, a third person will observe what really happens during the acting out of the case. Afterwards, switch roles in order to get the feel for both sides of the dynamic. Upon completing each case, the directee should express how he felt, whether or not he had been understood, whether he found the experience satisfying. The mock director, for his part, should explain how he felt and the third party can make observations from the outside.

In the bibliography at the end of this pamphlet, the director can find some basic reference books that explain in more detail these techniques and others.

"For God alone my soul waits in silence, for my hope is from Him" (Ps 62). When spiritual direction is conducted in an atmosphere of faith and prayer, silence will characterize the director. The silent guide is one who has not internalized the pressures of our society and who is not unconsciously seeking success, efficiency, control or competition with other directors. The director is the servant of God and he will be effective when he can say, "Here I am, Lord. I come to do your will." In the last analysis, he will not be able to discern the presence of God in the life of his directee unless God, Himself, opens his heart and his mind. Now it is easy to understand why so many directors begin their sessions with prayer to the Spirit.

VIII
"WHERE TWO OR THREE ARE TOGETHER, THERE AM I" — THE INTERVIEW

One spiritual director from St. Paul, Minnesota, gives a letter to his students before beginning spiritual direction with them. (See Appendix) In it he explains in part: "I try to be trinitarian in offering spiritual direction. What do I mean by that? I mean that from the Church's contemplation of the triune God, certain realities emerge that are worthy of our adoration and imitation. We learn that the Father, Son and Spirit are personal in their relationships; they hold each other as equals; they are distinct from one another; they are in deep perfect union with each other." (G. Keefe, in *Journal of the Midwest Association of Spiritual Directors,* Winter, 1974.) This is an important reminder, for the context of direction is God, Himself, and because of this the director takes care to create an atmosphere of trust, welcome and acceptance.

The spiritual dialogue participates in the mystery of God's own silence. There is something as private about direction as sacramental confession. Part and parcel of this is confidentiality, for the director who accepts privileged information ordinarily cannot use it in any other forum. Only a very serious situation would justify revelation, one in which a higher good for the individual or the community would be involved. As a rule of thumb, however, what is learned in the private dialogue should be treated with the same care as confession material. The directee, for his part, should be instructed that the director is speaking with him as an individual, in very private and concrete circumstances, that what is said here could be easily misconstrued in other situations. This means that he, also, assumes an obligation of secrecy out of respect for himself and for the director. Trust is a two way street, and the directee should be helped to merit trust.

This atmosphere of respect will be reflected in the director's concern for providing a comfortable place for the interview. It should be private, mirroring the type of intimacy that will be created. Likewise, the personal attitude of the director is important, for if he is tired, he will find it extremely difficult to give adequate direction, for he will constantly be looking forward to the end of the hour so he can go and have a beer. An uncluttered mind is the best thing for a listener.

Another indication of being "cluttered" is an overly busy schedule. If the individual who comes for direction feels that he is one of a series whom one is "fitting in," already the relationship is beginning on a strained basis. Spiritual direction should not be hurried, though it must be disciplined. Definite times should be established for each meeting, which ordinarily can be limited to one hour. For young people, half-hour interviews are ordinarily sufficient.

What we are saying is that from the start, the boundaries of the relationship should be established. What are his/her expectations of direction, and what are the director's? Why did he come to this director and not to another? What approach will be taken to reach the goals? How often will the meetings be and when? This clarity removes much uneasiness on the part of all concerned. It is also a way of testing the sincerity of those who are seeking direction, for their fidelity to the interviews is an indication of their willingness to face the pain of conversion, and the joy of breakthrough.

In the bibliography at the end of these reflections, you will find a reference to Fr. John McCall's *Counseling and Guidance during Retreat;* this is another must. In it he warns directors to be neither cold fish nor mother hens. No director should be so naive to think that he can direct everyone or even the same person at every stage of his development. In his relationship with the directee, the director must help him talk about himself, his feelings, his aspirations, his difficulties, fears and joys. It is not easy for some to open up on this level, so the director must have patience until defenses fall one by one. Social pressure, inability to relate with authority, shame, fear of being judged an odd ball — all form a wet blanket thrown over the person's deepest self. For this reason it is helpful to

— begin by getting to know the person, his/her name, interests, activities, family, friends
— present some matter on which he/she can react, such as the question of spiritual direction, some recent event, the challenges of life today
— see how he/she behaves with regard to the responsibilities of daily life.

Sometimes the inertia of the directee can be broken by the humor or challenge of the director.

In contrast, some directees speak very freely with little inhibition. Whereas this might be a positive factor, it could also be "smokescreen." Some try to snow the director so he will learn nothing about them. Eventually both the director and the directee will have to face the question: if this is a direction situation, what does the directee expect from it? There is no use prolonging unduly a relationship which deals simply with one's social self and never really getting down to a personal level and issues.

Others may come and begin talking about a precise fact or problem area in their lives. The adolescent may be all tied up in himself and extremely irritable because of it. Constantly referring everything to himself and torn apart by conflicting desires, he feels enslaved. Or a mature person may be facing life's difficulties as an adolescent. In any case, the director will have to touch the sore spot so that the poison can escape and the body can begin healing itself. Many will be seeking ready made answers. In some cases, answers and information must be given. But it would be extremely imprudent and unhelpful to dish out wise counsels unless one were sure of their utility to the directee. This means that the director must clear the ground with kindness and try to see what degree of human and emotional evolution the person has and what is the quality of his spiritual orientation at the present moment.

Since it is not necessarily advisable to say "yes" to a request to be one's spiritual director at the first interview, both director and directee should pray over the matter in order to get some perspective. It may be necessary to refuse a request. For example, if, as the relationship develops, some want to stay with trifles or want to constantly force the director into a know-it-all role, or who are consistently hostile, then there are clear reasons for termination of the nascent relationship. On the other hand, an interview can be considered functional if the following signs are present:

1. if the person talks about his past and present life and the feelings associated with his present situation and problems;
2. if he retells significant events in his life that have helped to shape his personality in the spiritual life;
3. if he expresses feelings toward anyone, past or present;
4. if he tries to understand his feelings, psychological defenses, weaknesses, strengths

and other factors influencing his relation with God and men.

On the contrary, if the following signs are present then the interview is not making the progress it should:

1. he spends too much time on present problems, repeating the same material;
2. if he digresses into neutral topics and wants to engage in purely social conversation;
3. if he engages in a repetitious and unconstructive area of resentment against one or more persons or situations which have harmed him or which he thinks have harmed him;
4. if silence has lasted for two minutes.

Fr. McCall adds that certain remarks can help the dialogue along, but they must always be purposeful: a *continuation remark* encourages the flow of expression. For example, the directee mentions the impression a prayer service at camp had on him. The director might say: "so the camp experience deeply influenced your prayer life?" Ordinarily the person will want to continue explaining how it did so. A *strengthening remark* supports or accepts positive suggestions which the directee himself arrives at. It emphasizes the fact that the individual must assume responsibility for his own life and that there is nothing wrong in doing so. *Explanatory remarks* are necessary at times for everyone needs information. But this must be done with all simplicity, using the words of Scripture as much as possible, and avoiding all technical jargon. Finally, there are *interpretative remarks* which help one increase his self-understanding. Interpretation is one of the most dangerous areas in spiritual direction, for it can so easily be made on lack of evidence. Actions can admit of various interpretations, so it is important to make remarks in response to one's story in order to clarify what a person really means and what underlies his actions. This is not to be done immediately; it requires time and love.

We are reflecting on a very important element of spiritual direction, communication. Much of what we have said is good advice for any counselor. There is, however, a certain specificity to spiritual direction as we have mentioned earlier. We can now turn our attention to other techniques which are helpful in initiating a relationship of spiritual direction.

Fr. Burke, a seasoned spiritual director from St. Louis, suggested three approaches which he has found helpful. The explanation of these may differ from his, but the ideas are basically the same as his. First, there is the *historical approach.* Some would like to go back in their lives in order to discover how they have been directly or indirectly touched by God. They can do so in a number of ways. For example, they can compose their own autobiography. Have them write about their family, their home and childhood, about school experiences and adolescence with its significant persons and breakthroughs. Encourage them to include significant events and persons in their lives, not omitting painful experiences nor accomplishments. This can be read through with the director. Or the director could suggest another model. He could use salvation history as revealed in Scripture as a model for personal history, and together with the individual could review these, relating them to his personal life's events.

Secondly, we can speak of an *existential approach.* This starts from where the person is at at this moment and move from where he is at each time. Here it is the director's task to help the person become more conscious of himself and of God acting in his life. In this regard, Fr. Aschenbrenner's "examen of consciousness" can be very helpful. The challenge of the religious way of living "is not simply to let the spontaneous happen but rather to be able to sift out these various spontaneous urges and give full existential ratification to those spontaneous feelings that are from and for God." How has the Lord been touching my life this day — this is the simple formula that helps us separate light from darkness. The practice of the presence of God, the use of the "Jesus prayer" or some other ejaculatory prayer, the establishment of a certain rhythm in one's life based on values one wishes to cultivate, are all excellent means of aiding a person in the development of an awareness of his present stance before God.

Thirdly, a director could use a *Christological approach.* In every conference one would zero in on the question "Who is Christ in your life?" Often it is helpful to suggest a theme which can be pondered over a two week period; this can be used to help one confront the question of how Christ touches his life. Some examples are: "Christ and faith," "Christ and hope," "Christ and friendship," "Christ and celibacy." These and other themes direct the individual's attention to Christ revealed in the Scriptures. When it is time for the conference, both director and directee share their faith-vision of Christ. This is not meant to become a progress report like report-card-days. It is simply a sharing of faith.

Other directors find it helpful to suggest the use of a *Journal*. In a way, this is a written examen of consciousness. The positive and the negative of one's days can be recorded in such a way that a real personal dialogue is initiated with oneself. Or a prayer journal might be tried in which one would jot down favorite quotations or insights 'from reading, the thoughts and ideas of others and finally one's own insights from the prayer and experiences of each day." Fr. Farrell points out that "writing creates an opening in the stream of consciousness and breaks up the automatic pattern of our life . . . writing is a way into what is going on and developing within ourselves." (See bibliography for references to Fr. Farrell's writings.)

Good spiritual reading of books or articles, or helpful tapes can be an excellent way to prepare for the weekly or periodic interview. Above all the director should have read the book or article which he suggests to his directee. In this way, both have something in common when they come together. Scripture should have a central place in his suggestions, but spiritual reading is not limited to it. Some novels, short stories or even some films might be more apt to open up dimensions of life at a certain moment than some explicitly "spiritual" book. Given this importance of reading, the director is obliged to keep an up-to-date list of real, solid material which can be suggested according to the various needs of his directees.

Closely connected with reading is the practice of meditation. Hundreds of books abound on this topic and meditation societies have almost become a fad in many parts of the country. They all have something important to say: we must learn to slow down, to distance ourselves from our over-involvement, we must learn to enter the world of the non-conceptual if we really want to know ourselves. Catholic tradition has a rich literature on meditation which is largely unknown. Some of these books are suggested in the bibliography. To get to the core of meditation, however, we can say that all methods require a) preparation. The presumption is that one's personal life-style will affect his prayer, that what he does immediately preceding his meditation will influence his meditation. When one comes before God, he must quiet down. This can be done in many ways: b) the body of the meditation. Meditation is an activity of the inner man. At the start the beginner will need something to meditate on. Here is where good books should be provided. Many uninitiated find it helpful to hear his director meditate out loud to get some idea of what happens in one's inner space; c) the conclusion can be very simply an act of thanksgiving, a plea for help, a decision for the future. Inevitably questions that the director will have to deal with are the frequency and the length of these periods, the time of day when they are done, the place, and the position of the body during the meditation. His own prudence and experience will enable him to deal with each individual according to his needs.

We are aware of the criticism of past spirituality which attempted in practice to create an inner world which was somehow other-worldly and therefore out of contact with the "real" world. Too often meditation degenerated into introspection. It is precisely because of dangers such as this that the spiritual dialogue is so necessary. Some people find it easy to over-intellectualize everything. He or she is always analyzing and categorizing and is consequently incapable of abandoning himself to a situation. Once he has mastered a situation intellectually, he loses interest in it. Another counter-productive attitude is that of excessive self-observation. In this case the person is condemned to be his own spectator; since he or she is so self-conscious, he is incapable of loving.

The spiritual director attempts to help the person become present to all that he or she is before God. To the degree that the person does move in that direction, to that degree will he or she lose life and find it. Self-preoccupation and worry will cede to greater concern, interest and respect for the Other. The director will provide tasks to be done until that time when the individual can pass from self-reflection to a more balanced orientation to the other. By setting tasks at the start, the individual will feel that something is happening, that the interviews are going somewhere. If possible the tasks should be suggested by the directee, but often that will not be possible and the director will have to assign something such as a reading, a meditation, a journal, a good deed.

IX
THE CORE OF DIRECTION

"Direction can be defined as the help that one man gives to another to enable him to become himself in faith." This definition from J. Laplace's *Preparing for Spiritual Direction,* (another *must!*) sums up well what the director is trying to do. Our spiritual tradition teaches us that the Spirit works in our lives and that we have "spiritual senses" which can be developed through exercise. Those who have developed it are called "wise men." The wise man has spent much time with God in silence and has come to see life from God's point of view; because of his patience, he has received the gift of spiritual discernment.

Discernment is a key word in direction and no one becomes himself in faith until he develops this capacity. Just to allay the fears of the uninitiated — discernment is not simply a Jesuit technique. Discernment is as old as Scripture; it was practiced by the Fathers of the desert and all the spiritual masters throughout the centuries. It is to the credit of the Jesuit Order that they have preserved, developed and refined the patristic teaching and made it available in modern dress.

Discernment, in the Christian interpretation, is "the process by which we examine in the light of faith and in the connaturality of love, the nature of the spiritual states we experience in ourselves and in others. The purpose of such examination is to decide, as far as possible, which of the movements we experience lead to the Lord, and to a more perfect service of him and our brothers, and which deflect us from this goal." (from another book you should have on your shelf, E. Malatesta, et alii, *Discernment of Spirits.*) This definition by Malatesta, explains precisely what a director is trying to do.

He is involved in a process which requires time, knowledge, judgment, patience, and continuity. In the process, his spiritual life and that of the directee touch each other and slowly a new spirit is born within which both will see more clearly what God wants.

"In the light of faith." To remember this is to remember the fact that God has initiated a personal dialogue with each individual and that each will be as unique as that person is unique. The spiritual director is at the service of the individual's dialogue with God; the director does not determine what that dialogue will be, but he is able to be like the friend of the bridegroom who rejoices in his friend's possession. On the other hand, the director's expertise in theology and his own faith life will steer the directee away from those paths where God cannot be found, in sin, in romanticism, in destroying human nature, and will keep him rooted in the reality of love.

The "connaturality of love" has a double dimension. First of all, and Laplace stresses this very much, the director must love his directee, otherwise all his talk about God's love will be in vain. "A spiritual father . . . must help him discover what it means to exist for someone . . . The affection of the natural order that he then shows, if it is real and true, is the best preparation for the spiritual relationship, the nature of which is still unknown to the seeker in spite of his desire for it." Secondly, a connaturality exists between both director and directee because both share the love of God which is the Holy Spirit. Because of this love both grow in sensitivity to the movements of God in the spiritual direction situation and in daily life.

Lastly, the definition speaks of examining the "spiritual states we experience." Many things go on within our minds and within our hearts. Our lives are filled with desires, feelings, projects, and thoughts. Not all of these come simply from the sensory, vital or psychic levels of our beings, for it is known that some arise out of our capacity for transcendence. God reveals himself in a way that we are capable of recognizing his action, so it must be through what we can discover in ourselves. Discernment is concerned with self, what is of God and what is not of God.

Along this line, I heartily recommend the excellent article by William J. Connolly, S.J., "Noticing Key Interior Facts in the Early Stages of Spiritual Direction" (*Review for Religious* XXXV/1976, p. 112-121). His key idea is that we must "notice" the movements of God's initiatives and our responses as they are revealed in our life of prayer. When someone seeks spiritual direction, he or she is developing a recognition of spiritual identity which is the first step toward mature awareness of self before God. Spiritual identity and the recognition/articulation of that identity, of one's relationship with God, are the first steps in discerning the direction of one's life. "Once he begins to realize who he is before God, he will also see that there is something wrong with him." This growth in "noticing" may take a long time, and it is better to allow it to develop than to impose a false self-identification that is purely intellectual.

How God is encountering him and how God is not encountering him are two elements of equal importance. What are the person's true feelings with regard to these pleasing and displeasing experiences of themselves before God? How does one feel and react to the experience of "nothing"? What does this do to his or her "idea" of God? Are they led beyond the idea to the Person? The director, in discernment, must zero in on actual facts, and not so much on why these things happen. By reflecting these facts back to the directee, he is enabled to articulate with greater clarity his or her own very personal reactions to self-before-God.

At other times "deep fear, anger, sadness or guilt are uncovered by dryness." These "have to be discussed at some length before the person can accept them sufficiently to begin to recognize them for himself and express them to the Lord. "Do you listen to the Lord when you prayer?" "Are you telling Him how listening to Him makes you feel?" Any feeling is worthy to be expressed to the Lord in prayer as the psalms amply prove: "Is it but in vain that I have kept my heart clean?" "Now that I am old and gray, O God, forsake me not" "Has God forgotten pity? Does he in anger withhold his compassion?" "Why, O God, have you cast us off forever?" "You have plunged me into the bottom of the pit . . ."

These feelings, the very stuff of discernment, are part of the person's real life. They may also arise from the pain of the world, from injustice, rejection, suffering, failure or oppression. One's religious experience is not foreign to these negative emotions; no matter what our society says, these are real to the person and to deny them would be to deny a rich dimension of prayer and participation in the Incarnation of the Lord. Connolly wraps up the attitude that must be taken by saying: "Is he willing to notice what is happening in prayer and in his life, or is he screening out material that conflicts with a mood he feels he must maintain?" "My emotional reactions to Him will be basically the same as the reactions I would have to human beings who affected my life as I feel God has."

Therefore the process of discernment is immersed in the real — real facts and real feelings about these facts. Feelings prompted by spiritual reading, feeling stirred up by life itself. All of these are revelatory of one's relationship to life and to God, to his or her ability to go beyond self into new realms of personal integration.

X
GUIDANCE IN PRAYER

There are two major ways to test the growth of an individual in the spiritual life. Morally, is he or she growing in love within the context of the real world? Psychologically, is the person growing in integration of the intellectual dimensions of faith and the emotional? Or to put it in other terms, is the individual growing in prayer? It is impossible to discern the Spirit of God without prayer. One of the director's main tasks will be to help the person grow in prayer.

In Harvard Square, Cambridge, there is the Center for Religious Development. "People come to the center for a variety of reasons, but for most the basic one is that they have heard that they will be helped with their prayer." How can a director help someone learn how to prayer so that he or she can begin to "notice" God acting, and themselves acting, in their hearts? William A. Barry suggests that the director take an "empirical approach" ("Spiritual Direction: the Empirical Approach" in *America,* April 24, 1976, p. 356-358). A good director will start from the individual's actual prayer experiences, or attempts at prayer. "How have you been praying?" God has been revealing himself to the person for a long time before he or she met the director. Many have difficulty maintaining themselves present to the all-present God. Chances are, however, that they also have a difficult time maintaining themselves present to many other things in life.

To develop the capacity to "be present to," a director will suggest that the directee begin noticing what is around him: waves, stars, cool night. Gradually attention can be drawn to Scripture: "what do you notice? what strikes you?" Rather than aggressively pursue prayer with surefire methods, the directee is advised to allow what is there enter into his or her field of consciousness and heart. The reactions in a person's life "are prayer, i.e. responses to the Lord who has loved us first."

Essential to growth in prayer is the clarification of what one really wants. A spiritual director is one who helps people clarify what they really want. "It is not easy to know what one really wants of God." When one works this out in life and with a director, the result is a growth in "realness." "The relationship to the Lord is like any other relationship, only more so: it thrives on reality and honesty . . . The task of the spiritual director is to help another stick with that relationship, to try to be more and more real, to ask with trust for what is wanted, to bear the pain of self-revelation." Growth in love for one's whole self goes hand in hand with growth in love for God.

There are certain means that can be suggested for growth in prayer. With no desire to prioritize, we mention the use of vocal prayers. At times people are helped immensely by reflecting on prayers they knew when they were young: the Our Father, Hail Mary, Act of Contrition. Repeating these prayerfully, using the rosary or apart from it, can be a strong aid to developing a sense of presence to God. Some, but not all, can use Sacred Scripture. What Barry says about prayer equally applies to the use of the Bible: "Resolutions to pray more, unaccompanied by good experiences of prayer, were like water in sand" which I paraphrase: "Resolutions to read and pray over scripture, unaccompanied by good experiences of Scripture with the director or a group, will be like water in the sand." The director could read and pray over Scripture with the directee in order to model an approach that could be used by him in private.

Ejaculatory prayers are certainly not out of style. The resurrection of the Jesus prayer and the *mantras,* show how powerful these types of prayer can be in developing one's presence to self and to the Lord. The director could well suggest ejaculatory prayers taken from Scripture if the directee cannot think of any of his own; "My soul is longing for the Lord," "My God and my all," "Ask and you will receive," "You are the Son of God."

Meditative writing is helpful for some. After writing down a familiar or beloved Scripture verse, the person is directed to continue by writing whatever comes into mind. This is one way of personalizing the word of God — or the teaching of the Church — and of combining work (ministry) and prayer. The writers of the Bible wrote their prayers; this exercise is in that tradition. This can also be done in a group. The way I have done it is to bring the group together for one half hour in silence and recollection. During the second half-hour period they are asked to write whatever comes to their minds, which can then be shared by those who wish in the third half-hour period.

Spiritual reading is a time honored way of nurturing the prayer life, used by the Church very effectively in the breviary. A certain amount of care should be used with beginners so they will not be seduced by the extraordinary (miraculous) or the penitential. Each spiritual director should have at his fingertips a number of spiritual books he or she can suggest according to various needs and gifts.

Another useful method for growth in prayer is the "weekly letter" from the director who includes therein a select Scripture verse upon which the directee can meditate. A variation of this is the "Word of Life" practiced by the Focolare movement. Each month a special saying from Scripture is chosen for a whole group. During the whole course of the month, this "word" is "examined for its most varied applications through continual contact with life" and is then shared in order "to build up our own interior life" as Chiara Lubich says in *The Word of Life* (New City Press, 1975). "Love your neighbor as yourself" or "he who humbles himself will be exalted" are two sample words which each member of the group uses as a password for the month, which are repeated over and over again, which form the matrix against which one's daily experience is examined.

In order to learn how to prayer, people have to participate in good prayer experiences. For this reason the director should initiate prayer with the directee in order to model the use of Scripture or spontaneous prayer. But the directee could also be encouraged to pray with someone, one other, or with a group which shares prayer. One caution should be made so that the directee will not develop an aversion to more structured and impersonal prayer, such as the Office or the Morning and evening prayers of a community. These are different ways of prayer; they do not have different value.

Silence is a necessary condition for prayer and interior silence can only be developed in period of exterior silence. "In silence we face and admit the gap between the depths of our being, which we consistently ignore, and the surface which is untrue to our own reality. We recognize the need to be at home with ourselves in order that we may go out to meet others not just with a mask of affability but with real commitment and authentic love" (T. Merton). Days of recollection are good times to introduce directees to silence.

At another time the director might want to suggest a prayer pilgrimage. Ordinarily one makes a pilgrimage to a shrine. In lieu of a shrine, one might be suggested to *walk* to the parish church in a prayerful spirit. Along the way they should keep their eyes open for all the manifestations of God's goodness and man's needs. When they arrive at the church, they can spend some time in prayerful adoration either before the blessed sacrament or the stature of some saint who is meaningful to them. The walk back home should be done in a spirit of gratitude and renewed commitment.

Song, dance, art, literature — all these can be great helps for growth in prayer in the hands of a skilled director.

XI
DIRECTIONS OF DIRECTION

Not all the literature in spirituality today presents a totally balanced picture of the spiritual life. Once again we feel it is helpful to "sort out" what we see in our society which is available for directors and directees.

Certain authors develop the subjective dimension of spirituality more than others. Ordinarily these writers are either psychologists, phenomenologists, or directors who use discernment as a primary tool. Thanks to these writers the feeling dimension of life has been recovered along with a strong emphasis on personal responsibility and self-determination. Because of their close analyses of spiritual experiences, these writers have also recovered for us the positive value of negative feelings and experiences. Three examples will demonstrate this approach.

Henri Nouwen's book *Reaching Out* is perhaps the finest available example of the subjective approach. His starting point is the person's experience of loneliness, hostility and illusion. With a deft hand Nouwen analyses how each of these operate in the life of an individual, and shows how the spiritual life arises out of this very "stuff" of life. "Wounded healer" is an apt description of the Christian, a title which dispels any illusion of angelism.

Adrian van Kaam is less unctuous in his use of the phenomenological method, but he is also rather subjective. He looks at the real experiences of the person and tries to discover within them the possibilities for growth and the impediments to growth. Eugene Kennedy is a writer of the same type.

Those who are strong on discernment of spirits

are concerned with discovering within the very fabric of man's psychology the spirits which reveal God and those which uncover the devil: thoughts, desires, feelings, temptations. We have already spoken of the fathers of the desert, we can also mention the abundant Jesuit literature in this vein.

Other authors stress the objective pole of spirituality with precious few pretensions to psychology. Of course, directors of this type cannot neglect the interior states of the individual, but their main concern is to present Jesus Christ, the beauty of God, the teaching of the Church and the ongoing revelation in Word, Sacrament, Neighbor and Situation. Rather than spending a lot of time analyzing causes or effects of loneliness, this type of director constantly directs the seeker's attention to concrete involvement in the work of the kingdom. Rather than analyzing the particular, these directors try to create vision for they believe what Bro. Giles of Assisi once said: "He who does not see great things, will think that small things are great." Laying great store on fidelity to one's state of life, moments of evaluation and introspection are kept to a minimum. "All of Christ's faithful . . . whatever be the conditions, duties and circumstances of their lives, will grow in holiness day by day through these very situations [of daily life], if they accept all of them with faith from the hand of their heavenly Father and if they cooperate with the divine will by showing every man through their earthly activities the love with which God has loved the world" (LG 41).

A few examples of prominent spiritual writers will demonstrate this pole. Louis Bouyer's *Introduction to Spirituality* devotes much time to the Word of God within the Church. All spirituality draws life from one's response to God revealing himself within the Church. "We must relive interiorly the entire history of the people of God."

Thils, a theologian from Leuven, wrote the manual *Christian Holiness.* In it, Christ, faithful fulfillment of the duties of one's state, the general means of sanctification (liturgy, sacraments, prayer), and one's social condition, are explained as the central elements of spirituality.

Sudbrack, writing in the authoritative *Sacramentum Mundi,* describes spirituality as "the personal assimilation of the salvific mission of Christ by which each Christian is always in the framework of new forms of Christian conduct and is comprised within the fundamental answer of the Church to the Word of salvation." Similarly, Hans Urs von Baltasar in an article entitled "The Gospel as Norm and Test of All Spirituality in the Church" writes: "The inner meaning of the Gospel demands that man imitate Jesus in such a way that he stakes everything ultimately on this one card, abandoning the rest of the pack. He must leave everything, without looking back, without trying to create a synthesis between Jesus and leaving one's home, between Jesus and burying one's father, between Jesus and anything else. He must "take up his cross," that is, he must put the fulfillment of God's will before any other personal plans, preferences or attachments . . ."

Dalrymple, in *Theology and Spirituality,* shows how the dogmatic facts of the Christian faith determine the pattern of the Christian life for the latter is the response to the former. Once this is clearly and forcefully understood, he considers man's point of view: what must one do to be a faithful son of God? Finally, Chiara Lubick, foundress of the Focolare movement, is very much oriented toward the objective pole of spirituality, in particular toward the "word of life." "Why must we go looking for the truth when the truth lives embodied in Jesus, the God-man? . . . to listen to the Word of God within us . . . and to put into practice one Word of God . . . for a certain period of time . . . And then the fruits would be communicated not only among ourselves, but also with [others] . . ."

The social thrust of many writers is a strong new element in spirituality best represented, perhaps, by *Soundings: A Task Force on Social Consciousness and Ignatian Spirituality.* "International justice or injustice is not 'one problem among others' in today's world; it must be grasped as 'a fundamental context, a characteristic of every problem.' In this regard it is in order to quote Pope Paul VI in his "Call to Action":

> The Spirit of the Lord, who animates man renewed in Christ, continually breaks down the horizons within which his understanding likes to find security and the limits to which his activity would willingly restrict itself; there

> dwells within him a power which urges him to go beyond every system and every ideology. At the heart of the world there dwells the mystery of man discovering himself to be God's son in the course of a historical and psychological process in which constraint and freedom as well as the weight of sin and breath of the spirit alternate and struggle for the upper hand . . . The dynamism of Christian faith here triumphs over the narrow calculations of egoism.

The Pope is calling all directors to free direction from the constant danger of turning the person in upon self. His call would have direction free the person to stand upright in the real world as it is and to take whatever concrete action would be necessary. This is a good corrective for a spirituality that tends either to be too subjective or too objective. Spirituality must not be separated from the situation.

XII
BIBLIOGRAPHY

Direction and Spirituality

A. van Kaam, "Dynamics of Spiritual Self-Direction," *Spiritual Life* (Winter, 1975), p. 261-282. This is an exceptional article which gives a bird's eye view of van Kaam's psychology and theology. It should be read in conjunction with his book, *In Search of Spiritual Identity* (Denville, New Jersey: Dimension, 1975). His approach can be understood by reading A. van Kaam, *Existential Foundations of Psychology* (Doubleday Image Book, 1969).

G. Braso, O.S.B., *Liturgy and Spirituality* (Collegeville: Liturgical Press, 1959). Though written before Vatican II, it contains the best of the theological developments which led up to and were included in the Council's teaching.

The interested director might also want to consult the following: L. Bouyer, *Liturgical Piety* (Notre Dame: University of Notre Dame Press, 1955); R. Guardini, *The Church and the Catholic and The Spirit of the Liturgy.*

Four Basic Models

D. Fleming, S.J., "Models of Spiritual Direction," *Review for Religious* XXXIV (1975/3), p. 352. Fleming Dulles' *Models of the Church* for his development. My approach is different, but we both touch common bases.

CARA Seminary Forum. 1234 Massachusetts Ave., N.W., Washington, D.C. 20005.

E. F. O'Doherty, M.A., Ph.D., *Vocation, Formation, Consecration and Vows* (Staten Island: Alba, 1971). A remarkably clear book of vast proportions which has many helpful insights for those in formation work.

Group Direction: Institutional Director/Spiritual Father

Documents of Vatican II, "Decree on Priestly Formation" 2,5,8; "Decree on the Appropriate Renewal of Religious Life," 18; "Decree on the Ministry and Life of Priests," 11.

J. Harrington, "The Ministry of Direction," *Priest* 29:25-32, (March, 1973).

Instruction of the Sacred Congregation of Seminaries . . . to the Bishops of the United States, May 26, 1928.

D. Isabell, *The Practice and Meaning of Confession in the Primitive Franciscan Fraternity* (Distributed by Franciscan Herald Press, Chicago).

E. Larkin and G. Broccolo, editors, *Spiritual Renewal of the American Priesthood.*

T. Merton, *The Wisdom of the Desert* (New York: New Directions, 1960); "Manifestation of Conscience and Spiritual Direction" *Sponsa* 30: 277-82 (July 1959); see also p. 249-54 (June 1959); "Notes on Spiritual Direction" *Sponsa* 31: 86-94 (November 1959); *Spiritual Direction and Meditation* (Collegeville: Liturgical Press, 1960).

Surrounded by a Cloud of Witnesses

This entire section is based upon F. D. Sackett, O.M.I., *The Spiritual Director in an Ecclesiastical Seminary,* (Canada: University of Ottawa Press, 1945).

For those interested in this history from a broader perspective, I suggest J. T. McNeill, *A History of the Cure of Souls,* (New York: Harper & Row "Torchbooks," 1951).

Another broad overview of the history of spiritual direction can be obtained by reading K. A. Wall, "Direction, spiritual" *New Catholic Encyclopedia,* Vol. IV, pp. 887-890.

Good, also, is F. Wulf's article on spiritual direction in *Sacramentum Mundi,* Vol. VI, pp. 165-167.

Jump Right In

Not all directees have the same degree of moral development. On this see D. Gibeau, "Kohlberg's Six Stages of Moral Development," *National Catholic Reporter,* 10: 9, (August 2, 1974); A. McBride, "Moral Education and the Kohlberg Thesis,"

Momentum, 4: 22-27, (Dec. 1973); L. Kohlberg, "Indoctrination vs. Relativity in Value Education," *Theology Digest,* 21: 113-119. (Summer, 1973).

See also Milton Mayeroff, *On Caring,* (New York: Harper & Row "Perennial Library," 1972).

H. Nouwen, *The Wounded Healer,* (New York: Doubleday, 1972), is excellent.

Counseling or Spiritual Direction: Woe is Me!

This chapter is heavily dependent on a series of unpublished lectures given by Carolyn Gratton, of The Institute of Man. There is much literature available on the topic. Here are a few suggestions:

A. Godin, "Spiritual Life and Mental Health," *New Catholic Encyclopedia,* Vol. 13, pp. 582-87.

E. Kennedy, "Counseling and Spiritual Dircetion," in *Catholic Theological Society of America Proceedings,* Vol. 18: 117-123 (1963).

W. Kraft, *The Search for the Holy,* (Philadelphia: Westminster, 1971). More recently Macmillan has published another book by Kraft entitled *The Psychology of Nothingness,* which is an analysis of the negative experiences of life and their role in personal growth. The author is also preparing, according to the grapevine, another book applying these ideas to religious life.

J. Laplace, *Preparing for Spiritual Direction,* (Chicago: Franciscan Herald Press, 1975). The great value of this book is that it does not approach the question from a theoretical viewpoint, but rather from an extremely practical down-to-earth approach growing out of his experience. It is the most basic book on spiritual direction that is available in English.

A. Van Kaam, *Religion and Personality,* (Doubleday Image Book). Because of the breadth of the small paperback, I suspect the new spiritual director would profit greatly from reading it. Van Kaam moves so ably in the field of psychology and direction, that he carries one along into a vision that is extremely helpful. One might be disturbed by his lack of integration around Jesus Christ, and the action of the Spirit, or by the terminology of his existential phenomenology, but this should not stop one from reading this.

Two somewhat old but standard books on dealing with health problems in spiritual direction are:

John C. Ford, *Religious, Superiors, Subjects and Psychiatrists,* (New Press, 1963).

R. Biot and Galimard, *Medical Guide to Vocations,* (Newman Press, 1955). This is an area that must be studied more in depth today. Frequently we never even mention the personal hygiene in our conferences, and yet many "problems" in spiritual direction arise from disordered physical or mental life. Hopefully, more help will come to us from experts in this field.

A basic, no-nonsense book on vocational discernment is R. Hostie, *The Discernment of Vocation,* (London: G. Chapman, 1963); more complex is L. Rulla, *Depth Psychology and Vocation,* (Chicago: Loyola, 1971).

A Tender Trap

I have already mentioned Van Kaam's book, *Religion and Personality,* which deals with transference in a broad context, as I have tried to indicate in my text.

I hope you will still be able to obtain A. Godin's *The Priest as Counselor,* (Techny, Ill. 60082: Divine Word Publications, 1968), which develops his idea of the priest as mediator. As you can see from my remarks in the text, his treatment of transference is very down-to-earth. If this book is not attainable, one should at least read his article "Transference in Pastoral Counseling," in *Theology Digest,* 9: 78-83 (1961).

Draw the Water from the Fountain Within (Jn 4, 14)

Much contemporary research and some exercises in listening skills have been compiled in a handy workbook entitled *Supervision — Lessons in Supervisory Skills.* This is the work of Fr. Isidore Langheim, who is currently trying to apply some of these skills to various forms of spiritual direction. More information is available by writing him at 3140 Meramec St., St. Louis, Mo. 63118.

Most texts used for training counselors explain other techniques available to those who wish to develop their capacity for understanding other people. One of the finest is, H. Clinebell, *Basic Types of Pastoral Counseling,* (Nashville: Abingdon Press, 1966). Good resource book.

The director has seen by now that most of the effort of spiritual direction is spent preparing oneself to be truly a "servant" of the Spirit. He may find the following articles helpful in his personal life:

Carlson, "Spiritual Direction and the Paschal Mystery," *Review for Religious,* (May, 1974) 532ff.

Connolly, "Appealing to Strength in the Spiritual Director," *ibid.,* (Sept., 1973) 1060ff.

Fleming, "Beginning Spiritual Direction," *ibid.,* (May, 1974) 546ff.

Leach, "Growing Freedom in the Spiritual Director," *ibid.,* (July, 1973) 834ff.

D. O'Rourke,"Model for the Confessor," *Priest,* (Feb., 1973) vol. 29, pp. 46-54.

"Where Two or Three are Together, There Am I" — The Interview

Fr. G. Kefe, has put together a "reflection book to aid the seminarian in his personal development." Those interested in it can write him at St. Paul Seminary, St. Paul, Mn., and ask for a copy of his

Formation Models in a Seminary Community. It is a most useful tool for a spiritual director, for it brings together in a very concrete way many tested means of helping seminarians. I have published in the appendix a letter he distributed to those interested in spiritual direction.

A book useful for background in prayer is: J. Lotz, *Interior Prayer,* (New York: Herder & Herder, 1968).

Much of this chapter depends on J. R. McCall's *Counseling and Guidance During Retreat,* a down-to-earth application of counseling principles to guidance work. This can be obtained for $1.50, from: Rev. Thomas A. Burke, S.J., Program to Adapt the Spiritual Exercises, 144 Grand St., Jersey City, N.J. 07302. It would be worth your while to get on the mailing list, for it is a veritable storehouse of aid for spiritual directors.

Review for Religious is not just for religious, and it should be in every reading room. A few years ago it began collecting a bibliography for spirituality which covers almost every imaginable question that might come up. Furthermore, the articles are always of actuality and interest. Read, for example, E. J. Farrell's "The Journal — A Way into Prayer," in *Review for Religious,* 30: 751-56, (1971). In vol. 34 of *Review for Religious,* D. Fleming has an interesting article, "Models of Spiritual Direction" (May 1975, pp. 351-57), and Sr. Mary Pellicane, responds to it (Sept. 1975, pp. 809-810).

Another article on the journal was written by Bro. Chrysostom Castel, "A Report on a Progoff Workshop at the Abbey of Gethsemani: The Intensive Journal Method and Process Meditation," in *Monastic Exchange,* 5 (Summer, 1973).

G. F. Simons, *Journal for Life* (Life in Christ, 201 E. Ohio St., Chicago, IL 60611) is the latest developed resource for "discovering faith and values through journal keeping." It is very creative. See, however, P. Tournier, *The Meaning of Persons* (Perennial Library Paperback), p. 64-65 for a criticism of the journal approach.

One analysis of introspection has been done remarkably well by D. von Hildebrand, in his classical work on spirituality, *Transformation in Christ,* (Doubleday Image paperback). Everyone should read chapter four on "True Consciousness."

The Core of Direction

We have already mentioned the importance of Laplace's book, *Preparing for Spiritual Direction.* A more specific treatment of discernment of spirits from Scripture and tradition is E. Malatesta, et alii, *Discernment of Spirits,* (Collegeville: Liturgical Press, 1970).

Finally, we wish to recommend to our readers, participation in the activities of the National Federation of Spiritual Directors, which brings together members of the Eastern Association of Spiritual Directors, Midwest Association of Spiritual Directors, Southern Association of Spiritual Directors and the Western Association of Spiritual Directors. Information on your particular region can be obtained from:

Rev. George Niederauer
5118 E. Seminary Road
Camarillo, CA 93010

The Midwest Association publishes a *Journal* three times a year which deals with the problem areas in direction work, providing at the same time a number of current resources and a forum in which directors can exchange their programs and their views. A subscription costs $5.00 for one year, and can be obtained by writing to:

Fr. Frank Wittouck
Sacred Heart Monastery
Hales Corners, Wisconsin 53150

The *Cara Seminary Forum* has already published material on the seminary spiritual director. Back issues and subscriptions can be requested from:

CARA
1234 Massachusetts Ave. N.W.
Washington, D.C. 20005

APPENDIX

Letter to a Directee

Dear Friend in Christ,

Please accept this letter as an attempt on my part to offer an explanation of some ideals that I hold about spiritual direction. I would like to make it as personal as possible, personal insofar as I sense your presence while I write, personal insofar as I want to make transparent my thoughts about this sacred privilege.

I try to be trinitarian in offering spiritual direction. What do I mean by that? I mean that from the Church's contemplation of the Triune God certain realities emerge that are worthy of our adoration and imitation. We learn that Father, Son, Spirit are personal in their relationships; They hold each other as equals: They are distinct from one another; They are in deep, perfect union with each other; They are one.

Spiritual direction strives to reproduce these divine relationships in the human, but Spirit-filled, dialogue that occurs.

It is important that the communications be personal. We try to avoid generalities, abstractions, intellectualizing that render the communication imperfect and sterile. Both of us must strive to speak from our interior convictions or lack of them. We are not two computers exchanging information, but two persons trying to grow in faith and love together. Like Jesus in His post resurrection appearance to the Apostles, we want to exclaim, "It's really I."

For the relationship to be personal, we must adore and imitate the equality that Father, Son and Spirit celebrate with each other. Both of us must strive to overcome any feelings of superiority or inferiority that would damage the Trinitarian ideal we cherish. We must strive to accept our fundamental equality with each other.

When both of us do this we can enjoy certain relaxation. We do not have to put on pretences or airs, but simply be ourselves. We can have exchanges that are honest, humble, accepted. We are not threatened at all, because we see each other as equals. Our conversation at once has the encouragement that comes from an equal. We begin to fulfill the command of Christ: "Love your neighbor *as* yourself." When we avoid being above or below one another we can enjoy what it is to cherish another person as you do yourself. Equality makes this possible.

This equality is not sameness or blindness. This equality discovers, appreciates, and celebrates the distinctions that are present between us. The distinctions do not loom up as threats, but rather as cause for rejoicing as we recognize our otherness. Our differences of age, authority, position, talents, grace are not cause for fear or separation, but rather become stimulation and excitement to share in a complementary way our personal gifts. God's gifts are always meant to be shared, to become mutual, to build up the Body of Christ. Gifts that are isolated quickly diminish and vanish. Gifts that are shared increase and endure.

When we prayerfully strive to make our relationship reflect the personalness, the equality, the distinctions of Father, Son, Holy Spirit, we will begin to experience some of the joy that St. Paul felt in the counseling that he offered to others. It will unite us in Christ. It enables us to realize between ourselves what St. Paul expressed unabashedly to his people in statement of fact. "You have a permanent place in my heart" as well as his request, "Give me a place in your hearts."

If we have accepted the Trinity as the basis for our relationship, then we should strive to give expression to this in our dialogue. Paradoxically, I will often act as Son to you. What do I mean by this? I mean that just as the Son is the reflection, the exact likeness, the glory, the splendor, the word, the obeyer of the Father, so will I strive to be like that toward you. I will encourage you to be Father by initiating whatever thoughts, convictions you have about your life, and then I will strive to respond toward you with the same fidelity that the Son responds to the heavenly Father. I want to do this so well that you might exclaim in some silent, equivalent way: "This is my beloved Son in whom I am well pleased."

You can see yourself in me. I have become the reflection of you by my words. You have the privilege of seeing yourself mirrored in the faithful, attentive words of another person. This mirroring enables you to see yourself more objectively and clearly. The understanding, the acceptance that you receive by my response to you should bring delight even though in the process your flaws might become more apparent. The hope that I carry is that my response will help you to "become perfect as your heavenly Father is perfect." My being Son to you enables you to grow in the likeness of the Father, to strive, to become what Jesus was: "the exact likeness of the Father."

There are other times when I will act as Father to you. I will initiate thoughts and suggestions that seem to fit your life. In these moments, I then seek your response, your sonship, your word. I want you to recapture what I have said to you so that I know you understand. I will draw from experiences of my life, from my prayers, my reading, my studies to be a good father to you. I crave to see you accept what you behold in me and adapt it to yourself. I pray that the experiences of my life bear fruit in your life.

I know that both of us must grow in holiness together. Just as St. Paul was edified by the faith of his people, and his people were edified by his faith, so also do I feel that our faith should be mutually revealed and shared so that both of us mature in Christ, put on the mind of Christ, grow in the stature of Christ. In spiritual direction we stand together or fall together. There is no lukewarm middle ground.

There are different ways in which you might review your life in preparations for our visits together. John Wright, S.J., suggests the way of faith, hope, charity. Faith would cause you to discuss the prayer that you experience daily. Hope would suggest that you share your difficulties, sufferings, disappointments and failures with your spiritual director. Love would prompt you to focus your life on community. These are just organizational suggestions as obviously the three are intimately related and over-lap.

Another way of organizing a review is to consider word, sacrament, community and try to perceive your living of these ideals.

Still another way could be your contemplation of Father, Son, Spirit, to see how you respond to their distinct influence on your life. Did I reveal the Father by initiating, generating, creating, planning, providing? Did I reveal the Son by responding, obeying, articulating, reflecting, mirroring? Did I reveal the Spirit by animating, uniting, exciting, anointing, enlightening, comforting?

You may well develop some organizational procedures of your own. The main thing is that you obtain as rounded a view as you can about yourself.

This review you can make in moments of prayer or extract from your journal if you keep one.

Finally, I would like to suggest that at every spiritual level conversation we have that we pray together. We are trying to discern the mind of God. It seems proper that we approach God in prayer, seeking His blessing on our humble efforts. This should give an unction and direction to our dialogue that will make the total conversation prayerful and sanctifying.

I would also like to give you assurance that I will pray for you frequently, and by name, to our heavenly Father. I earnestly solicit your frequent prayers for me.

May the grace of our Lord Jesus Christ, the love of God and the fellowship of the Holy Spirit be ours together.

Sincerely, Fr. Keefe

(See *Review for Religious,* 33: 542-545, May, 1974. Originally published in *Journal Midwest Association of Spiritual Directors.*)

EXISTENTIALISM AND ITS IMPLICATIONS FOR COUNSELING .... .65
M. Emmanuel Fontes

A study in depth which leads to seven general principles for integrating existential insights into counseling.

THE CREATION OF FULL HUMAN PERSONALITY .... .65
Joseph Drew & William Hague

Complete psychological growth is a process inseparable from total reality—biological and spiritual, internal and external. Vocation is important.

SEX AND EXISTENCE .... .65
Adrian van Kaam

This booklet describes psychological, social and religious factors which hinder or promote the integration of sex and human existence.

NEW EDUCATIONAL METHODS FOR INCREASING RELIGIOUS EFFECTIVENESS .... .65
Dean C. Dauw

Special group methods of self-education that have proved helpful to others are also helpful to religious organizations.

LOVE AND SELFISHNESS .... .65
Alice von Hildebrand

True love cannot be separated from a joyful readiness to make enduring sacrifices for the sake of the beloved.

PERSONAL IDENTITY AND RELIGIOUS COMMITMENT .... .65
Francis Forde

Religious commitment calls for a mature judgement and consistent fidelity and creative care.

NEW LOOK CELIBACY .... .65
Rosemary Haughton

A vocation to celibacy is a sign of the Christian orientation toward the eternal life. This booklet reveals its larger dimension.

A PSYCHOLOGY OF THE CATHOLIC INTELLECTUAL .... .65
Adrian van Kaam

The split between secular and religious learning rooted in psychological history must be healed to prevent disaster.

EMOTIONAL DEVELOPMENT AND SPIRITUAL GROWTH .... .65
Timothy J. Gannon

To what extent can insights into a man's emotional life contribute to the solution of problems of spiritual growth.

LITURGY IN ADOLESCENT PERSONALITY GROWTH .... .65
Marygrace McCullough

The Liturgy does contain personality building forces that can be used effectively on the adolescent level.

PSYCHOLOGICAL DEVELOPMENT AND THE CONCEPT OF MORTAL SIN .... .65
Robert O'Neil & Michael Donovan

This booklet challenges the premise of current sacramental and educational practice that children can be guilty of mortal sin at the age of seven.

THE ADDICTIVE PERSONALITY .... .65
Adrian van Kaam

A psychological study of the origin, structure and function of the personality prone to addiction.

SPIRITUALITY THROUGH THE AGES .... .65

Our understanding of God and his love has shifting emphases. The contour and quality of our response will vary from time to time.

A PSYCHOLOGY OF FALLING AWAY FROM THE FAITH .... .65
Adrian van Kaam

A rare insight into this problem by a theologian with a psychologically oriented background.

UNDERSTANDING AND ACCEPTING OURSELVES AND OTHERS .... .65
William Zeller

Self-knowledge is important for mental health. Healthful growth of the individual depends on social development.

WHAT'S WRONG WITH GOD .... .65
Thomas M. Steeman

A probing search into a question that has practical ramifications for the modern man.

HELPING THE DISTURBED RELIGIOUS .... .65
E. F. Doherty

Like everybody else religious have problems of tensions and anxieties. Their causes and manner of handling are treated with sensitive insight.

WORLD POVERTY . . . CAN IT BE SOLVED? .... .65
Barbara Ward

In depth analysis of the problem of world poverty with sensible suggestions on how to solve it.

THE PRIESTHOOD: MASCULINE AND CELIBATE .... .65
Conrad W. Baars, M.D.

Psychiatrist, author, and consultant on the problems of the priesthood at the 1971 Vatican Synod of Bishops, Dr. Baars develops the positive values of celibacy and a regimen to achieve a priesthood both celibate and masculine.

THE RIDDLE OF GENESIS .... .65
Robert Koch

The study of comparative religion and modern biblical exegesis help to convey the essential message of the first eleven chapters of Genesis.

THE CHURCH TODAY .... .65

Important studies by men like Ratzinger, Schweizer, Congar, Pauwels and Winkhofer on various aspects of the Church in the modern world.

GROWTH TO MATURITY .... .65
Peter Cantwell O.F.M.

Maturity is not an accident of living. It is an achievement whose roots reach back to the very beginning of life, and are nurtured in successive stages.

THE DEFINITION OF THE CHRISTIAN LAYMAN .... .65
Edward Schillebeeckx O.P.

This author has established his right to speak with authority on a subject that is very important today. He bases his observations of Vatican II documents.

THE QUESTION OF FAITH IN THE RESURRECTION OF JESUS .... .65
Leonardo Boff O.F.M.

There have been many new interpretations of the Resurrection of Christ. These are investigated and contrasted with traditional belief.

HOW TO TREAT AND PREVENT THE CRISIS IN THE PRIESTHOOD .... .65
Conrad Baars, M.D.

A well-known psychiatrist, from vast experiences, discusses the role of the Church in the causation, treatment and prevention of the crisis in the priesthood.

FROM RESENTMENT TO GRATITUDE .... .65
Henri J. M. Nouwen

Challenges seminaries to overcome negative feelings and respond to life by a positive creative ministry.

THE MESSAGE OF CHRIST AND THE COUNSELOR $1.50
John Quesnel

An expert discusses the principles of counseling in general and pastoral counseling in particular as gleaned from the life of Christ.

TEMPTATIONS FOR THE
THEOLOGY OF LIBERATION .... .65
Bonaventure Kloppenburg O.F.M.

A member of the Papal Theological Commission warns against the various temptations to water-down, distort or belittle theology and the Gospel message. A clear voice in babel of confusion.

THE FAMILY PLANNING
DILEMMA REVISITED .... .65
John G. Quesnell

Since the publication of **Humane Vitae** a lot of study has been given to family planning. This booklet looks at the new insights in the light of the teaching of the Church. His is an optimistic approach.

RENEWAL AND RECONCILIATION .... .65
Reflections for a Holy Year
Msgr. James O'Reilly

The world, the Church, the family and society plus the sacramental system are discussed within the context of renewal and reconciliation. These reflections are appropriate for any year.

POLITICAL STRUGGLE OF ACTIVE
HOMOSEXUALS TO GAIN SOCIAL
ACCEPTANCE $1.50
George Kelly

Having learned from civil rights movements, overt homosexuals are exerting strong and expert political pressure to affect public mores.

CHARISMATIC RENEWAL IN
HISTORICAL PERSPECTIVE .... .65
John Carroll Futrell, S.J.

The Charismatic movement is recognized as good, authentic experience of the action of the Holy Spirit. The movement needs solid theology and orthodox biblical foundation. Risks are noted.

TO WHOM SHALL WE GO? .... .65
Zachary Hayes O.F.M.

Christ and the mystery of man is the theme of this booklet. It fills a gap as it focuses on the place of Christology in the Church today.

THE MORAL PROBLEMS OF CONTRACEPTION .... .65
Msgr. James O'Reilly

This booklet discusses the objective morality, without imputing subjective blame, of the contraceptive act. Contraception is regarded as a devaluation of a basic human good, namely the power to initiate human life.

COUNSELING TODAYS YOUTH $1.95
Peter Cantwell O.F.M.

With obvious expertise the author discusses the problems of modern youth and modern parents. He offers some practical suggestions in dealing with these problems.

THE SPIRITUAL DIRECTOR $1.50
Damien Isabell O.F.M.

This is a practical guide for spiritual direction on which growth depends. It contains an overview of approaches and an invaluable bibliography.

THE SACRAMENT OF PENANCE AND RECONCILIATION .... 65¢
Msgr. George A. Kelly

This is a sociological and historical study of the changes of attitude and practice of the Sacrament of Reconciliation.

THE HOMOSEXUAL'S SEARCH FOR HAPPINESS .65

Conrad W. Baars, M.D.

In this psycho-philosophical approach Dr. Baars treats homosexuality with remarkable compassion and understanding. He points out that the pressing need is personal, individual affirmation.

THE NATURE AND MEANING OF CHASTITY .65

William E. May, Ph.D.

Chastity is a loving integration of sex and affectivity into our lives enabling us, as sexual beings, to love and be loved. This definition is explained in detail.

LAY AND RELIGIOUS STATES OF LIFE: THEIR DISTINCTION AND COMPLEMENTARITY .65

James O'Reilly

The distinction between the lay and religious states of life must be maintained because of the nature of the movement of man toward salvation and the effect of the environment of life in the world.

THE PASCHAL MYSTERY: CORE GRACE IN THE LIFE OF THE CHRISTIAN .65

Augustine Paul Hennessy C.P.

Christian hope lies in the Risen Christ. Christians must learn to take on Christ's attitude toward the cross and the glory of it.

VALUING SUFFERING AS A CHRISTIAN: SOME PSYCHOLOGICAL PERSPECTIVES .65

Henry C. Simmons C.P.

Within the mystery of the cross of Christ, the sufferings of daily life hold meaning and value. Christian hope lies in the promises of Christ's death and resurrection.

SEX, LOVE AND PROCREATION .... .65
William E. May
This booklet is concerned with the important question: Can sexual intercourse as an act of love ever be separated from intercourse as a creative act?

AN UNCERTAIN CHURCH
THE NEW CATHOLIC PROBLEM .... .65
George A. Kelly and John A. Flynn
In a clear, concise manner this booklet explores the foundations of academic freedom. It is also a reaffirmation of the great Catholic heritage in intellectual circles.

MINIMUM ORDER $5.00